PRAYERS
OCCAS

Ian Black

First published in Great Britain in 2011

Society for Promoting Christian Knowledge
36 Causton Street
London SW1P 4ST
www.spck.org.uk

British Library Cataloguing-in-Publication Data
A catalogue record for this book is available from the British Library

ISBN 978–0–281–06367–3
eBook ISBN 978–0–281–06668–1

Typeset by Graphicraft Limited, Hong Kong
Manufacture managed by Jellyfish
First printed in Great Britain by CPI
Subsequently digitally printed in Great Britain

eBook by Graphicraft Limited, Hong Kong

Produced on paper from sustainable forests

Contents

About the author

Ian Black is Vicar of Peterborough, Canon Residentiary of Peterborough Cathedral and Rural Dean of Peterborough. Formerly, he was Vicar of Whitkirk, Leeds, and a member of the Chapter of Ripon Cathedral. He has served in parishes in Kent, was a Minor Canon of Canterbury Cathedral and has been a prison chaplain. Prior to ordination, he was a tax accountant. His previous books, *Intercessions for the Calendar of Saints and Holy Days* (2005) and *Intercessions for Years A, B and C* (2009), are also published by SPCK. He is married with two sons.

www.ianblack.org.uk

Introduction

————•◆•————

Prayers for All Occasions is a collection of original prayers covering a wide spectrum of subjects and situations. They have emerged from whenever there has been a need to collect together thoughts and hopes in prayer and will suit anyone who leads prayers in public or who is looking for a resource to enrich private devotions. They are all contemporary in style and resonance, being born out of twenty-first-century living and believing. There are biblical echoes, which those with detailed knowledge of the Bible will find enriching and those without will not be hindered by. Some have been written as a response to a particular situation with a particular person or occasion in mind. Some were written because I couldn't find the words elsewhere to capture what I wanted to express. Some are a personal response to facets of life today. I have not tried to substitute classic prayers, which have stood the test of time, and I have no desire to see them removed from use. As life moves on, though, there is a need to ensure that our praying keeps up with us.

The book is divided into eight sections to provide a loose wrapping for the contents. 'Through the year' covers the Christian year from Advent to the Feast of Christ the King. On the way it touches on all of the major milestones with a few additional ones reflecting the society we are in. So there are prayers for Hallowe'en and Bonfire Night, both of which display the starting point of our culture and therefore provide an opportunity for a Christian response. The prayer for 'Thanksgiving' points to an international perspective. 'Church and ministry' holds the prayers that broadly fall into church use or refer to the Church's concerns and ministry matters. The doors are opened more widely with 'Pastoral prayers', which responds to human living, confronting our mortality and some of the darker aspects of life.

'Community' brings together the worlds of education and work, volunteering and daily living. It is followed by 'Government and justice', which offers prayers for all involved in power relationships from royalty to the homeless. 'Home and family life' collects together prayers of blessing on homes, covenanted relationships, parenting and when things go wrong. Most relationships are sustained round the table and through hospitality, be it corporate or personal. The prayers for 'Food and hospitality' offer graces and thanksgivings. There are also prayers for chocolate, written on Easter Day surrounded by mountains of it, and for beer and wine.

The book ends with a 'Devotional prayers' section. These are prayers inspired by faith, hope and trust in God's gracious love. The prayer to 'Still my restless heart' is balanced by an invocation to be stirred for action. Sometimes we need to be still and know that God is God and sometimes we need to get up and act! Faith without works is dead and spirituality must be more than time-out therapy! 'Waves' is a prayer of trust in God. It comes from the thrill of being buffeted by the waves with a surfboard and refreshment on the beach. It bows with respect to St Cuthbert who prayed standing in the waves. He was made of sterner stuff than me: I need a wetsuit to emulate him. 'Ripon Jewel' is inspired by the seventh-century golden clasp discovered near Ripon Cathedral and which can be seen there. It provides an opportunity for us to reflect, when surrounded by so much precious metal in churches, on where our true treasure lies. A number of these prayers were written in the library of Ripon Cathedral, sitting next to this artefact.

There is an alphabetic thematic index in the back pages to aid with finding prayers quickly to suit an occasion.

These prayers are rooted in a deep faith and trust in God's grace. For me this is foundational. All is gift and in that lies our hope in Jesus Christ.

Ian Black

THROUGH THE YEAR

Advent

Come, Lord Christ,
to restore all that has been lost
through struggle and fear,
in sorrow and in pain.

Come, Lord Christ,
to restore the balance of hope
for those oppressed and hungry for justice,
overlooked and counted of little worth.

Come, Lord Christ,
to restore to wholeness
the image that is tarnished
with sin and shame,
neglect and distraction.

Come, Lord Christ,
in poverty and humility
to raise us to your eternal glory. Amen.

Christmas

Child in the manger
vulnerable and holy
born of a woman
adored by the lowly
sharing our frailty
to raise us to glory
in passion and rising
you transform our story.

Sent by the Father
through the power of the Spirit
fulfil our desires
this day and for ever. Amen.

Christmas shopping

God of generous love,
you give freely of yourself
in your Son Jesus Christ.
Bless us as we choose gifts
as tokens of love and affection.
Free us from losing the purpose
in the bags and wrappings;
keep us from spending more than we can afford
and from falling into debt.
Give patience among the crowds
to shop workers and customers alike.
May none be abused
in our preparations for this festival;
for we meet you in the stranger
in the high street as at your crib.
May the gifts we seek remind us
of those who knelt to worship and adore you
and inspire our own devotion,
for you are the source of life
and hope of salvation,
now and always. Amen.

Blessing of the Christmas crib

Loving Lord Jesus,
on this holy night*
angels sang in praise at your birth,
shepherds knelt to adore you
and Mary cradled you in her arms.
May this crib scene remind us that you are always with us
and bring us to worship you today and every day. Amen.

*'at Christmas' may be substituted for 'on this holy night' if
required.

New Year

Lord of time and eternity,
we stand on the threshold of a new year.
Strengthen our resolve
to dedicate our lives afresh in your service
leaving behind all that would distort your image within us
and lead us astray.
Keep us in peace,
guide us in justice,
sustain us through all this year may bring,
for in you is our hope and our salvation,
our lasting joy and fulfilment
through Jesus Christ. Amen.

Epiphany

Generous God,
everything we are and have comes from you;
in adoration we lay before you
the sweet fragrance of our worship,
for you alone are worthy of our praise and thanksgiving;
in service we lay before you
our money, power and choices,
for in your will we find true freedom and direction;
in trust we lay before you
our pains and longing for healing,
for you hold the goal of our lives' journey
and the hope of salvation
in Jesus Christ,
King of kings and Lord of lords. Amen.

Candlemas/Presentation of Christ in the Temple

Grant, Lord,
to the weary, rest,
to the longing, the glimpse of hope fulfilled,
to the expectant, the promise of grace dawned,
to the faithful, an honoured place
at the feast of your kingdom.
Bring us all, O Lord,
to rejoice in your salvation and glory,
now and for ever. Amen.

Ash Wednesday

Lord, you bring us from dust to life.
As our flower fades
may we know your peace.
In the wilderness, the city and by the seashore
may we know your presence.
In the market place and on the way
may we hear salvation announced.
Be with us through these forty days and nights
that we may grow in your love
and deepen in faith;
for you are our source and goal
and hold all that passes between. Amen.

Palm Sunday – palm crosses

With shouts of joy and jubilation
you entered your city, Lord Christ.
With shouts of anger and hatred
you carried your cross to your death.
With a cry you breathed your last
and bought for us salvation and peace.
May these palm crosses remind us that
while our love may be like the morning mist
that vanishes so early,
yours remains constant and true.
In this is our hope and confidence to stand before you.
Keep us faithful through times of trouble and peace,
and may we rejoice in your eternity. Amen.

Holy Week

In the Temple, Lord Christ,
you overturn our priorities and false rules
with the money-changers' tables.
In the house, Lord Christ,
you overturn our sense of respect and dignity
in accepting Mary's gift.
In friendship and betrayal, Lord Christ,
you overturn the boundaries of hospitality
in sharing food with Judas and those on the edge.
As we journey through this week with you
may we come to understand more fully
the transforming power of your love
and grow more in your likeness,
to your honour and glory. Amen.

Maundy Thursday

Forgive my presumption, Lord,
to sit and eat with you,
knowing the evil at work in my heart.
Forgive my hesitation, Lord,
to approach your presence,
knowing the lengths to which you have gone
to win this place for me.
Forgive my questioning, Lord,
of those alongside me,
knowing they too are the guests of your generosity.
May the hospitality of your love
fill all our hearts and shape our lives
for your glory. Amen.

Passion of Christ

Lord Jesus Christ,
we give you thanks and praise
for you endured the horror of the nails,
piercing your hands and feet,
the crown of thorns
adorning your head,
and you bore the beating and mocking
to our shame.
May your wounds bring true healing
as you gather,
in your suffering,
all whose nakedness is exposed
and who are treated as commodities to be exploited.
Forgive us when we do not know what we do
and when we do know.
Restore us in your saving glory. Amen.

Holy Saturday

In the silence of the grave, Lord Jesus,
you restore our life.
In the darkness of death,
you bring light to our grief.
In the destruction of the body,
you heal our brokenness.
In the dawning of the new day,
you shake the earth with a power no tomb can hold.
May we live in anticipation of your glory
and rejoice in your hope,
now and always. Amen.

Easter

Risen Lord,
in bursting from the tomb
you have broken the power of death
and we see there is no darkness
that can overcome your love.
Breathe into our lives
the wonder of your saving glory,
that our song may ever be
your alleluia. Amen.

Ascension

Risen Lord, you reign in glory.
Rule in our hearts and lives.
Mould our wills to your will
and bring every knee to bow
in humble adoration;
for you are one
with the Father and the Spirit,
holy and eternal. Amen.

Pentecost/Whit Sunday

Holy Spirit of God,
breathe into your followers
new life and confidence
as you did in the upper room.
Pour upon your whole Church
the gifts of your grace
that it may live and work
to your praise and glory. Amen.

Trinity

Eternal Source of life and love,
holding all in purposeful order,
awaken reverence and awe
for your mystery and wonder.

Eternal Presence,
making visible and intimate
the depth of your being,
draw all people into your outpouring heart.

Eternal Spirit,
indwelling,
moving creation into being
and hearts to leap for joy;
inspire justice,
excite truth
and refresh the face of the earth.

Father, Son and Holy Spirit,
Blessed and glorious Trinity,
to you be glory and honour,
now and for ever. Amen.

Corpus Christi/Thanksgiving for Holy Communion

Lord Christ,
on the hillside you shared bread
and the hungry were fed;
in the upper room you broke bread,
poured wine
and invited your friends to remember;
by the seashore you provided fish
and the ashamed were restored for your service.
As we gather round this table
may this sacrament feed us for our journey,
unite us in action
and inspire us to be generous
as you are generous.
May we taste and see
how gracious your love is. Amen.

Seedtime and harvest

Good Lord,
your rich bounty provides for our needs
and sustains our lives.
Bless us in our stewardship of the earth
in preparing the ground for sowing,
tending the crops
and bringing the harvest home,
that there may be enough for all your people
to rejoice in your goodness;
through Jesus Christ. Amen.

Hallowe'en

Blessed Lord,
in the darkness of our fear,
may your light shine.
In the presence of evil,
without and within,
may your goodness prevail.
In the chaos of lives distracted,
may your Spirit bring order and direction.
In the turmoil of destruction and hate,
may your peace descend.
In the grip of death,
may your redeeming will raise to new life.
For Christ is Lord of all
and in his victory is our hope and salvation. Amen.

All Saints

God of holiness,
you send your Spirit into our hearts
and by your grace we participate in your love.
Make our lives shine with the radiance of your glory
that we may choose life over death,
hope over despair,
freedom over bondage,
and rejoice in your blessing for all creation,
through Jesus Christ. Amen.

Bonfire Night

God of truth and love,
on this night
as sparks ignite a flame
and the sky is lit up by flashes and sparkling,
so may the example of the saints
burn and explode within us
that our hearts may delight
in your love and glory.
Forgive the divisions
that would breed hatred and violence.
Strengthen all who build bridges to unity and peace
and give us grace
to trust in your promises,
rejoice in your love
and work for your Kingdom alone,
now and for ever. Amen.

Remembrance

God of hope and consolation,
we hold before you all who have died
as a result of war,
and those who continue to carry the scars
of injuries to body or mind.
May we remember the cost,
lest we forget the value of our freedom,
the responsibilities it brings
and the sanctity of peace.
Sustain us in our building of communities fit for heroes
and where all can flourish,
to your honour and glory. Amen.

Victims of war

Lord Jesus Christ,
you gave yourself for our salvation
through your death on the cross;
raise all who have fallen through violence and warfare.
Give to grieving hearts the comfort of your love,
heal the divisions that divide and destroy,
and grant peace to build anew
for your glory and the good of all. Amen.

Peace

Spirit of God,
breathe into our hearts
peace that is content in your love.

Spirit of God,
unite us in honouring
the gift we are to each other.

Spirit of God,
give nations common cause
to strive for justice and the welfare of all people.

Spirit of God,
fill us with your grace
to trust in your promises
and accept your forgiveness for ourselves and others.

Spirit of God,
breathe into the whole of your creation
the peace that comes from you alone
through Jesus Christ. Amen.

Christ the King

Lord Jesus Christ,
in you we see the splendour of God in human form,
sharing our joys, sufferings and frailty.
In your resurrection and ascension
we see your majesty completed
and are silenced in wonder.
May we find in your service true freedom
and in your will our hopes fulfilled;
for you are one God with the Father and the Spirit,
and live and reign in eternal glory. Amen.

Bible

Lord God,
you reveal yourself in each generation
through word and sacrament,
visions and songs,
timeless knowledge and new discoveries.
Open to us the pages of your truth,
revealing treasures not yet understood
and wisdom forgotten.
Challenge us with the call of your justice,
the breadth of your love
and the mystery of your will.
Ignite in our hearts a flame
to delight in your liberating truth;
through Jesus Christ, the Word made flesh among us. Amen.

Blessed Virgin Mary

Lord Jesus,
in your mother, Blessed Mary,
we see a model of devotion
and willing acceptance
of your will and call;
fill us with your grace
that we may bring to birth
the fruit of your love
and follow in your steps
in passion and glory. Amen.

Thanksgiving

Voice 1*   When the hungry are fed and the thirsty given drink
Response   We give you thanks, O Lord.

Voice 1   When the strangers are welcomed and knowledge
           is shared
Response   We give you thanks, O Lord.

Voice 1   When the homeless are sheltered and nakedness is
           clothed
Response   We give you thanks, O Lord.

Voice 1   When the sick are cared for and healing is dispensed
Response   We give you thanks, O Lord.

Voice 1   When the lonely are befriended and the outcasts
           embraced
Response   We give you thanks, O Lord.

Voice 1   When hatred is banished and fear dispelled
Response   We give you thanks, O Lord.

Voice 1   When homes are filled with love and lives are
           nurtured
Response   We give you thanks, O Lord.

Voice 1   When your peace reigns and hope is triumphant
Response   We give you thanks, O Lord.

**Voice 1 can be shared among a number of people, especially
when used in a larger group.*

CHURCH AND MINISTRY

Gift of music

God, the source of life and joy,
we thank you for the gift of music,
its uniting of different voices in one song,
its stirring of the depths of the heart in praise.
Fill us with this vibrancy
that our lives may rejoice in your love
and be renewed in the Spirit's hope, now and always. Amen.

Before a concert (1)

Lord of all creating,
we dedicate to your glory all our music making.
As the notes soar so may our hearts rise to heaven
and echo with your praise.
May we be united in one true harmony
that all may find cause to celebrate your freedom
and the earth resound with a symphony of your love;
through Jesus Christ, your Son, our Saviour. Amen.

Before a concert (2)

May the music of our praise
and the vision of your glory
combine to inspire our thoughts and actions
making an acceptable offering in your sight,
O Lord, our strength and our redeemer. Amen.

Before a concert (3)

God of trumpets and harps,
cymbals and song,
we thank you for the gift of music.
May those who listen and those who perform
be so moved by the rhythm of your creation
that our hearts may dance in your praise;
through Jesus Christ our Lord. Amen.

Before a Eucharist (1)

Eternal God,
we gather to celebrate
[the saving life and death of your Son]*.
Be present among us in the breaking of bread,
and bring us at the last
to share in the eternal banquet of your love;
through Jesus Christ our redeemer. Amen.

*The words in square brackets may be replaced by the name
of a festival.

Before a Eucharist (2)

Sanctify, O Lord, our hearts and minds
and inspire our praise,
that as we celebrate this sacrament
of your loving presence among us
we may be transformed in your heavenly glory;
through Jesus Christ our Lord. Amen.

Coming to worship

Faithful and loving God,
as a shepherd cares for his sheep,
so you love and care for us.
We come to this house of prayer
to sing your praises,
to hear your holy word spoken
and to ask your forgiveness for our sins.
Fill our hearts with your gracious love
that our lives may tell of your glory
in Jesus Christ our risen Lord. Amen.

Drawn to loving service

Loving God,
as a mother embraces her children,
you draw us into the fold of your love.
As the Father of our Lord Jesus Christ,
you hold all your creation in your everlasting arms.
Fill our hearts with love for you,
that loving you we may serve you
in Jesus Christ our Lord. Amen.

Servant Church

Lord our God,
whose Son taught his holy apostles
that those who would be great must first be servants,
give to your Church this servant heart,
that any glory we seek will be to your name
and our triumph only in the cross of your Son.
May no act of love come to be regarded as beneath us.
We ask this in the name of the one who humbled himself
to reveal your saving presence among us,
Jesus Christ our Lord. Amen.

Christian service

God, the source of light and hope,
in your grace we thank you for your love,
which guides us through storm and calm.
Illumine our course,
inspire our vision
and ignite our passion
for your service,
in Jesus Christ our Lord. Amen.

Spiritual renewal in the Church

Lord of our pilgrimage,
we give thanks for all whose compassion and energy
helped midwife the birth of Christianity in this land.
So inflame us with the same spirit of discipline and love,
that in our own generation your Church may be enlivened
to sing your praises in words and acts of loving service.
In the name of the ever-fruitful Three,
Father, Son and Holy Spirit. Amen.

Christian unity

Lord Jesus Christ,
you call a rich tapestry of people to follow you
and challenge us with a new commandment
to imitate your love.
Give to us the gift of your grace
to fulfil this calling with joy and gladness,
that the world may rejoice in your praise.
Make us one as you are one
with the Father and the Holy Spirit,
eternal Trinity, now and for ever. Amen.

Before a meeting

Be among us, Lord Christ, as we meet in your name.
Inspire all who speak to enlighten our understanding.
Give patience to all who listen to discover fresh treasures.
Expand our horizons to behold your dawning Kingdom,
and grant us the gift of your grace
to trust in your providence,
now and always. Amen.

Small groups

Lord Jesus Christ,
you said that when we gather together in your name,
however many or few we may be,
you will be in the midst of us.
Be present with us now
as we open your word,
delight in your truth
and glory in your name.
Inspire us with wisdom,
excite us with passion for justice,
and send us from this place renewed in faith
that our lives may honour you
in all that we say and do;
for you are one with the Father and the Spirit
in all eternity. Amen.

Church's mission and ministry

Lord Jesus Christ,
on the mountain top you gave your disciples
the great commission
to continue your work of reconciliation
and to draw all people to you,
to baptize and teach them in your way.
Bless us who are sent in your name.
Give us your grace
to be open to the questions that struggle to find expression,
the thirst that is unsure where to be refreshed
and the hunger that is scared to ask for bread.
Guide us as we seek to uncover the path of life and peace.
Shield us from the pride of disdain and contempt
that would think itself better than anyone else,
for all are equal in your sight,
and the treasure for which you died;
to the glory of the Father, through the Holy Spirit. Amen.

Men and women in ministry

God of Abraham and Sarah,
Moses and Miriam,
Peter and Mary of Magdala,
you call men and women to witness
to your love and covenant in each generation.
Open our hearts to the guidance of your Holy Spirit.
Free us from the chains of the past and present
that impede your gospel
and give us courage to trust in your providential care.
Lead your Church
to strive for justice,
uphold dignity
and rejoice in all your gifts of grace,
to your honour and glory. Amen.

Vocation

Prepare me, O Lord,
for the place you have set for me.
Use me as you will,
for in your desire is my hope
and in your purpose is my true goal.
Give me patience
when your pace seems too slow to me.
Strengthen and sustain me
when I fear that I may collapse under pressure.
In all things, keep me hopeful and keep me thankful,
for your love has held me to this point
and I know it will never let me go.
Forgive me when I forget your eternity;
through Jesus Christ who is our companion and salvation.
Amen.

Global Church

Lord,
your Spirit sends apostles
to all points of the compass,
and you draw people of all races and nations
into one family in your Church.
Broaden our horizons to learn from one another,
expand our generosity to support one another,
increase our vision to pray for one another,
that united as joint heirs of your grace
the whole earth may resound
with your praise and glory,
through Jesus Christ,
who is our true peace. Amen.

Stewardship thanksgiving

Generous God,
your loving grace fills the whole world with your goodness.
Help us to see the gift in all things,
that with thankful hearts
we may be generous in turn with all you give to us.
Help us to see that as all things come from you
so they find their true fulfilment
when offered in your service;
through Jesus Christ our Lord. Amen.

Fundraising

Generous God,
you set before us everything we need
to delight in your blessing.
Save us from greed that would hoard only for itself.
So fill us with your grace that resources may be shared,
that none may go hungry
where others have more than they need,
your temples be in ruin while others enjoy luxury,
the sick be passed by while others protect status.
Teach us to give willingly from the first-fruits of our labour
for your honour and glory. Amen.

Welcoming as Christ

Give to us, O Christ,
your grace to welcome all
as if embracing you,
for in strangers angels have been met.
Bless us in our encounters with others,
and may our hospitality
be a treasure to lay before each guest,
for in serving them we serve you.
May the generosity of your love overflowing
bring us all to delight and flourish in your peace. Amen.

PASTORAL PRAYERS

Before taking Holy Communion to the housebound

Be present, Lord Jesus Christ,
as I take this Holy Sacrament
to those unable to gather at the altar
through sickness or infirmity.
As they are fed with your Word
fill them with your grace,
enfold them in the fellowship of your Church
and remind them of your eternal love,
that they may rejoice in your salvation;
for you are one God
with the Father and the Spirit,
now and for ever. Amen.

Going into nursing care

Lord of all our days,
you hold our life from birth to death
and bless us in each stage.
Be with us in this new journey.
In our letting go,
keep us thankful;
in our embracing of the unknown future,
keep us hopeful;
in our being cared for,
keep us graceful.
May we know your blessing
in our new surroundings
and among those with whom we will share this home.
Refresh our faith and trust in your unfailing love
and the promise of your salvation
in Jesus Christ. Amen.

In hospital or a hospice

God of compassion,
by the wayside, next to pools,
in the house and amidst the crowd,
your Son healed the sick
and restored them to wholeness.
Bless all who are in hospital or hospice.
May they know your love for them
and feel the warmth of your presence in their hearts.
Strengthen the fearful,
calm the anxious,
bring peace to all who are troubled.
Restore our faith in your unfailing goodness
for you hold our lives
as in the palm of your hand
and will never let us go;
through him who brings healing in his wings,
Jesus Christ our Lord. Amen.

Accepting our own mortality

Give me humility, O Lord,
to accept the limits of my own mortality.
Give me your Spirit, O Lord,
to face it with hope and courage.
Give me your presence, O Lord,
to know that in all things
you are before me and above me.
Give me your peace, O Lord,
to see and welcome the gift in each day.
Surround me, O Lord,
with your love
and protect me from falling into despair,
for you are the source and goal of all existence,
and through Jesus Christ, our salvation and true joy. Amen.

Terminal illness

Christ, who prayed in agony in the garden,
knowing your time had come,
be with all who stare into the darkness of death.
May they find the light of hope.
Fill their hearts with peace
and save them from dying unprepared.
Set at rest the guilt of sin,
that trusting in your redeeming love
they may come to share
in the joy of your eternity,
through you, Jesus Christ our Saviour. Amen.

Anxiously watching and waiting

Watch and wait, dear Lord,
with all who keep vigil
by the side of someone they love;
to their anxiety bring peace,
to their fear bring hope,
to their tears bring your loving embrace,
for all our lives are held
in the purpose of your love
and look to the joy of your salvation
in Jesus Christ. Amen.

Brother Death

Brother Death,
you stand at the threshold of eternity
bringing release and liberation from suffering.
May we be prepared for your coming
and greet you without fear.
Bring us to the peace that comes
with the fulfilment of Christ's promises
and to the glory of our heavenly home,
through Jesus Christ who is our resurrection and our life.
Amen.

Embracing the darkness of death

Lord Jesus,
in your death you plunged the depths
of loss and despair
and embraced the darkness.
As we die with you,
so may we be brought to the table of your mercy
and the glory of your eternal home. Amen.

Parents' loss of a child

Blessed Lord,
whose mother's soul was pierced
by the heart-wrenching pain
of watching her son die on the cross,
be with all parents whose hearts are broken
by the loss of their child.
In the darkness may your light dawn,
revealing that no life is wasted in your love
and all are held in your embrace.
May the tears that flow become a well
and the emptiness be filled again
with praise and thanksgiving,
for you bring life out of death
and hope out of despair
in Jesus Christ. Amen.

Funeral

Lord of life,
in the hope and trust of your Son Jesus Christ's resurrection,
we lay before you *N*:
for all that was good and inspiring in his/her life
we give you thanks;
for the love shared and the memories treasured
we praise you;
for the injuries and hurts he/she endured
and any inflicted –
intended or not –
we ask your forgiveness and healing mercy.
We entrust him/her now to your eternal keeping,
for you hold all souls in life
and in your redeeming love
is our hope and salvation,
through him who died and rose again for us. Amen.

Tragedy

O God, your Son Jesus Christ wept over Lazarus his friend,
and heard the anguished cries of Jairus for his daughter;
hear those whose lives have been marked by tragedy
and whose hearts ache with grief.
Console those whose world has been shattered
and whom no words can console.
Comfort them in their darkest hour
with the assurance that nothing can
separate us from your love.
Raise the dead to new life
that all may again sing songs of thankfulness and praise,
to your honour and glory. Amen.

Anger

Take my anger, Lord, lest it consume me.
Keep me from the hardness of heart
that wills violence and death.
Preserve me from the bitterness
that destroys from within and pollutes my soul.
Hear my cry of pain and despair.
Pour upon me such grace
that I may work as a channel of your justice and peace,
and open up in the storm
a clearing for your healing and transformation,
through Jesus Christ who is our peace. Amen.

Child protection

Lord Jesus Christ,
be with all who work to safeguard children.
May they themselves be protected from being damaged
by the images they see
and the stories told.
Enfold in your loving arms those injured,
whose trust has been destroyed.
Calm the fury of those incensed and outraged.
Forgive the evil that springs from past pain and abuse.
Give to offenders the courage they need
to confront their actions.
Make your light dawn on the darkness of sin
and bring to us all your healing and restoring grace;
for in you is our hope and salvation. Amen.

Coping with abuse

Lord Jesus,
you were mocked and beaten,
taunted and isolated
by those who should have upheld justice.
Be with all who are abused
and whose dignity is violated;
whose trust is betrayed
by acts of violence and humiliation.
Restore them to wholeness of mind,
free them from the anger and shame
that destroys from within,
and build them in the love
that is life-giving and life-affirming,
to the glory of the Father. Amen.

Conflict and disagreement

Lord, your searing judgement
penetrates the hidden places of our hearts and minds.
Heal the injuries carried that would wound others,
confront the prejudices held that would restrict vision,
calm the fears that would strike those who challenge.
Transform us in your grace with humility and love,
for the sake of him who died to bring true peace. Amen.

Confronting evil

Spirit of God,
strengthen me
in the darkness of this hour.
Purify my heart
that I may know my need
for your forgiveness and mercy.
Surround me
with your protection
that no evil may assault my soul,
but I may trust in your prevailing goodness.
For the darkness is not dark to you
and the night is as bright as the day.
Let your light flood the shadows and hidden places,
bringing stillness and peace
to all that is troubled,
in Jesus Christ, our risen, ascended and glorified Lord. Amen.

Being sent to prison

God of mercy,
you know the secrets of our hearts
better than we do ourselves;
give us* a penitent and contrite heart
to face the evil we* have done
with honesty and remorse.
May we* use the time ahead
to turn away from sin
and rebuild our* lives on your sure foundations
that we* may learn to walk once more in your ways,
live with respect for ourselves* and others,
and with humility accept the help we* need
to take our* place in society
as people of blessing and peace,
through Jesus Christ
our redeemer and guide. Amen.

*To put the prayer into the third person, replace 'us' with 'those convicted of crimes' or 'they', with consequent adjustment throughout the prayer.

COMMUNITY

Education Sunday

Bless us, O Lord, in our teaching and learning.
Give to enquiring minds wisdom and understanding.
Inspire us all with your justice and peace
and bring us always to delight in your truth;
through Jesus Christ our Lord. Amen.

New school year

Lord Jesus Christ,
we stand at the beginning of a new school year,
fresh and full of promise.
May the temples of young minds
be nurtured with the quest for understanding
and the discovery of the wonders of your creation.
Set those who belong to this community
on firm foundations,
that they may flourish in mind, body and spirit,
and grow to contribute to a society
in which all benefit. Amen.

End of a school year

Heavenly Father,
thank you for this school;
for friendships made,
all it has given to us
and all we have been able to give to its life.
Bless us in these holidays
and in the new beginnings that await us [next term];
through Jesus Christ our Lord. Amen.

Examinations

God of wisdom and understanding,
strengthen all who are anxiously facing examinations.
In testing give them all they need to do themselves justice.
In preparing give them the diligence
to focus on the goal ahead.
Keep their perspective balanced
that the stress may prove no more than needed
to be equal to the task,
and in all things may they know your love for them
which is not dependent on performance or grades;
through Jesus Christ. Amen.

Assessing and marking

Awaken within me, O Lord,
respect for the efforts before me to assess.
Create a space within me
to honour the fruit of study,
however serious or careless it may seem.
Open a channel within me
to give credit for all that can be affirmed,
and to point to growth where improvement is needed.
Direct my heart to your justice
with fairness and impartiality,
for you are the God of truth and love,
now and always. Amen.

Starting at university and college

Lord of new beginnings,
you open fresh opportunities
for us to grow in your truth and understanding;
be with all new students
as they go up to universities and colleges
for the first time.
May they flourish in friendships and studies,
have their minds expanded
by ideas and knowledge,
and develop into the people of stature
you would have them be;
through Jesus Christ. Amen.

Students

In the Temple, O Christ,
you debated with the teachers
and amazed them with your understanding.
On the hillside and by the seashore
you taught all who came
and astounded them with your authority.
Bless all students
in their quest for understanding
and pursuit of knowledge.
May they delight in truth,
grow in wisdom
and shape the world for the greater good of all people,
for with the Father and the Spirit
you are to be praised and honoured,
now and always. Amen.

Industry and manufacturing

Lord Jesus Christ,
you learnt a trade with Joseph in the carpenter's workshop
and knew the value of making with your hands;
bless us in our industry,
our sharing in creation
through manufacturing and commerce.
In our trading strengthen the bonds that unite
and open the opportunities to share
new understandings and developments.
Keep us mindful of the impact on the environment
that we do nothing to harm it
or the people and species which depend on it;
to you be honour and glory,
now and for ever. Amen.

Industrial disputes

Jesus,
friend of fishermen and leaders,
tax-collectors and officials,
men and women,
owners of business and hired workers,
we bring to your grace and mercy
disputes in the workplace.
May your wisdom inform discussions and negotiations,
your light shine on the disagreements and grievances,
and your justice reveal a path to resolution
for the good of all;
for you bring true peace and harmony
to all who trust in you,
now and always. Amen.

Financial and economic concerns

Lord Jesus Christ,
you called rich and poor alike
to trust in you
and not in treasures that can be lost or stolen;
teach us to regard money
as a tool for use in your service
and not as an object of devotion;
to harness it for justice and relief
and the benefit of all.
May our hearts be moved
by your generous love
which shares of its very self
for our benefit and salvation.
Give us grace to be filled with hope and your goodness,
now and always. Amen.

Agriculture

God our creator, redeemer and sustainer,
you set us in a world abundant with produce
and give us skill to till the soil and harvest crops
to support our life;
bless all who work the land
and manage the countryside.
May they protect the environment from damage,
the earth and rivers from pollution
and livestock from cruelty.
Inspire our trading with your justice
in fairness of price and wage.
As we are thankful for your rich bounty,
so may we ensure that none go hungry;
through Jesus Christ our Lord. Amen.

Sail the seas

Eternal Father,
whose Son Jesus Christ
stilled the storm,
directed the catch
and travelled from shore to shore,
bless all who sail the seas
transporting goods,
harvesting for food,
travelling or seeking peace.
Protect them in danger,
comfort them in isolation and lonely hours,
and bring them to the surety
of a haven on earth and to come;
now and for ever. Amen.

Volunteering

Lord God, you call everyone to follow you
and to give freely of their time and gifts.
Bless all who respond to your generous love
through voluntary service in the church
and wider community.
May the lives that are transformed
be enriched by these signs of your grace in action,
and be stirred to songs of thankfulness and praise
for your outpouring of love through human lives;
to the honour and glory of Jesus Christ
our inspiration and Saviour. Amen.

Overseas aid and work

Generous God,
your servant Joseph administered aid
to the starving who journeyed to Egypt for food,
and you inspired the first followers of your Son
to send relief to the church in Jerusalem in their need;
give us a compassionate heart
for all who suffer as a result of natural
and human-made disasters.
Bless those who give their skill to humanitarian relief,
who show your love in care and dedication to the poor.
May we share your rich bounty
with joy and thanksgiving
using our skills to assist development work
with rejoicing and gratitude;
for all good gifts come from you
and we share freely as we have received;
through Jesus Christ. Amen.

New job

Guide me, Lord,
as a new venture unfolds before me.
Give me wisdom
in the challenges I have not faced before;
give me humility
to learn from those whose experience shared is a blessing;
give me patience and understanding
with everything that is not as I would have wished,
and inspire me with vision to work to change
anything that needs to be transformed and renewed.
In all things may your will be done
and your kingdom come. Amen.

Redundancy

Lord, you call everyone to follow you
and give us gifts to use in your service;
be with all who have lost their jobs and seek paid work.
Hold those who are anxious about making ends meet
and feel frustrated at loss of position and place.
Open opportunities for talents
to be channelled constructively,
that dignity may be restored,
hope renewed
and none feel they are without worth or value,
for in your sight all are a unique act of your creation
and purpose
and in your love we flourish,
now and always. Amen.

Retirement

Lord of time and eternity,
you set the seasons for life to flourish.
As we approach the autumn of our work
we give you thanks for the years of labour,
colleagues we have joined on the way
and contributions made.
Open new avenues
along which gifts may be used
and new discoveries made,
that we may continue to grow in your love
and abound in your hope,
through Jesus Christ our Lord. Amen.

Internet

Spirit of God,
proceeding from the Father
through the Son,
uniting in truth and love,
breaking down barriers
and connecting people in thought and will;
thank you for the internet,
its power to share ideas, news,
and bring people together.
May it open for us
a channel of your transforming grace.
Forgive the ways it is corrupted
through malicious intent and exploitation.
Expand our vision
and set us free to delight
in this wonder of your creation
that our hearts may be inspired
to action for your glory. Amen.

Travel

Lord Christ,
be with all who travel
by land, sea or air.
As they journey keep them in your love.
May their way be guarded and protected from all evil.
Guide their going out and returning,
for you are our true destination
and the pilgrimage which directs the course of our lives,
now and always. Amen.

Weather

Lord God of the universe,
you set the seasons to enable the earth to yield fruit
and provide for life to flourish.
As the sun warms and ripens the crop,
may it not scorch or burn;
as the rain waters and flows in rivers,
may it not flood or drown;
as the snow and frost blanket the earth,
preparing for new growth,
may they not overwhelm or engulf.
Be with all who suffer
when the forces that sustain life
also threaten and bring our fragility to the fore.
In all things may we know
your blessing and salvation
in Jesus Christ. Amen.

GOVERNMENT AND JUSTICE

For the town/city

God of life and love,
we pray for our city*.
Grant us peace in our communities,
honesty in our trading,
hospitality and warmth in our welcoming,
integrity in our planning and civic life,
that the common good may prevail
and your kingdom of righteousness and justice be affirmed.
We ask this in the name of Jesus Christ,
who is the way, the truth and the life. Amen.

*Or 'town', 'district' or 'village'

Before an election

God of justice and compassion,
leaders and outcasts came to your Son
and were received with the same love:
for those easily brushed aside he made space;
of those with much, much was expected;
to the penitent he offered forgiveness;
for all, the new life of his kingdom was announced.
Hear our prayer for those standing for election
to serve and represent all people
of this constituency in parliament*.
May we use our vote wisely for the common good
and pursue that peace in which all can delight;
through Jesus Christ our Lord. Amen.

*'Ward' and 'council' may be substituted respectively for
'constituency' and 'parliament'.

Integrity in politics

God of justice and truth,
you set the standard for leaders to aspire to.
Give to those whom we elect
honesty in their dealings,
dignity which extends to all
and a desire to strive for the common good,
that all people may rejoice in your liberty
in Jesus Christ our Lord. Amen.

Government

Lord, whose majesty is above the heavens,
guide with your Holy Spirit
those who hold the highest offices of state.
Give them wisdom
as they struggle with the concerns of the day.
Strengthen them to do what is right
and save them from everything that would corrupt the will.
Bring us to that day
when we shall dwell in your courts
in righteousness and peace;
through him to whom is owed true allegiance,
now and always. Amen.

Freedom and democracy

Lord of justice and peace,
we thank you for the freedoms we enjoy
to choose our leaders
and shape the course of our common life.
Give us wisdom to use the power we share
for the good of all,
the relief of those in need
and the furtherance of wholeness and truth;
through Jesus Christ. Amen.

Journalists

God of truth,
bless all who tell the stories
and share the news
of the events of our day.
Give them courage when exposing vice,
wisdom when calling to account,
compassion when in the presence of tragedy,
and balance when controversy and dispute rage.
Guard them against becoming cynical,
but sharpen their wits to lies and deceit.
Keep them hopeful and faithful
in the values of your Kingdom,
that their outlook and goal
may be guided and directed
by justice and integrity;
through Jesus Christ our Lord. Amen.

The Queen

King of kings and Lord of lords,
hear our prayer for Elizabeth our Queen
and all who share with her
in the government of this country.
Bless her in those she meets
and the authority committed to her charge.
May she be an instrument of your peace and justice
that this nation may proceed in unity and concord
and be a beacon of hope to the world,
through Jesus Christ the Prince of Peace
and the source of true glory. Amen.

Armed forces

Michael, Archangel,
your sword blazes with terror
scattering the forces of evil
and bringing them to tremble beneath you.
Inspire the armed forces with this passion for what is right.
Strengthen those who battle evil,
restraining excess,
and defending the innocent.
Keep them always mindful of the image of God in all people.
May what must be done be carried out swiftly and decisively.
Finally, forgive us the failure that led us to this hour,
and give determination to rebuild
for the honour and glory of Jesus Christ. Amen.

Facing the battle/deployment

Lord, our strength and stay,
fortify us as we face this hour.
Give us courage for the battle ahead.
Keep us alert to the dangers unseen.
Watch over us
that we may ever be held
in your protection.
If I fall this day,
may my hope and trust
be in your salvation and mercy;
for you guard us in life and in death
in Jesus Christ. Amen.

Police

Surround with your protection, O Lord,
all members of the police as they protect our communities.
Defend them that they
may always act justly;
when force is necessary
may it be proportionate;
when falsehood is confronted
may dignity be upheld;
when fear and pain are met
may your compassion direct their actions.
In all things keep them from losing faith
in your goodness in humankind,
and sustain them for your love's sake. Amen.

Ambulance service

God of compassion,
bless all members of the ambulance service
as they go to the aid of sick and injured people
without judgement of circumstance or cause.
Give them strength to face the traumas they meet,
empathy for the distress encountered
and skill to assist as required;
for in caring for the patients in their charge
they embody your loving service to neighbours in need;
through Jesus Christ our Lord. Amen.

Fire and rescue service

Lord, you came to our aid as our Saviour.
We thank you for all in the fire and rescue service
who emulate this self-denying love
in risking their own lives to save others.
Bless them as they respond to calls for help
and advise on safety.
Strengthen them as they face danger
and scenes of suffering.
Keep them ever under your protection;
through Jesus Christ our Lord. Amen.

RNLI

Lord Jesus Christ,
friend of fishermen,
bless all who risk their lives
for the safety of others
through the Royal National Lifeboat Institution.
We give thanks for their bravery,
dedication and selfless service to all in peril on the seas.
Strengthen and sustain them in danger's hour
and bring them home in safety and peace;
through Jesus Christ. Amen.

Suffering through injustice and oppression

Heavenly Father,
hear our prayer for all who suffer through oppression,
the hatred of prejudice, or violence.
Keep us from the indifference that passes by on the other side,
and the bitterness that breeds further evil.
Fire us to strive for the dignity of all to be honoured,
and for the reformation of those
whose cruelty enslaves and injures,
that your kingdom of justice and peace may be furthered.
We ask this in the name of him whose cross
has become the symbol of our redemption and freedom,
Jesus Christ our Lord. Amen.

Refugees

Lord Jesus Christ,
you had to flee from Herod's wrath
and became a refugee in Egypt.
Look with compassion on all who flee
violence, oppression or natural disaster today.
Expand the charity of host nations
to find the resources to meet their needs.
Inspire hope instead of hatred
and faith instead of fear,
that all your children may rejoice in your peace;
to the glory of God the Father. Amen.

Homeless

Lord of the highways and byways,
whose compassion flows with grace and mercy
and whose Son Jesus Christ
gave dignity to all whom he met,
raise up the broken
and help the routeless rediscover direction.
Send your Holy Spirit to challenge the full
to ensure the hungry are fed,
the destitute sheltered,
and all are greeted with love;
through the same Jesus Christ our Lord. Amen.

Poverty

Lord Jesus Christ,
you blessed the poor
with the promise of the Kingdom of heaven.
Keep us from using this to excuse injustice,
complacency and exploitation.
Forgive the conditions set up by human greed,
which exclude and ensure unfairness
in trade and access to the earth's bounty.
Challenge the hearts of all
to work as they are able
for the relief of need,
release from bondage
and the ending of oppression;
that your Kingdom may come
on earth as in heaven
for the benefit of all people. Amen.

Environment

Spirit of God,
who moved across the waters,
bringing life from the elements of that first dust,
lead us to respect your world,
inspire our stewardship,
forgive our wanton destruction,
turn our foolish exploitation,
and give us wisdom to live in harmony
with the earth's rhythms and natural balance;
to the glory of the one who is our beginning and our end,
now and always. Amen.

HOME AND FAMILY LIFE

Blessing a new home

Bless, O Lord, this home
that it may be a place of rest to refresh,
of hospitality to delight in good company,
a space to be, to know and feel secure.
Keep in peace all who dwell here
and send them out to live to your praise and glory. Amen.

House blessing

Bless to us, O Lord, the door
that it may guard our going out and coming in.
Bless to us, O Lord, the kitchen
that the fruits of your bounty
may be prepared with gratitude and generosity.
Bless to us, O Lord, the table
that around it we may be sustained
with nourishment and company.
Bless to us, O Lord, the chairs
that we may rest and delight in conversation.
Bless to us, O Lord, the television
that it may inform and inspire our imaginations.
Bless to us, O Lord, the bed
that it may be a place of rest and intimacy*.
Bless to us, O Lord, the bath and shower
that they may cleanse and revive.
Bless to us, O Lord, the roof
that it may provide shelter and security.
Bless to us, O Lord, all that is housed here
and everyone who dwells within these walls.
All for your love's sake. Amen.

*'Intimacy' may be replaced by 'safety' if more appropriate.

Relationships – commitment and civil partnerships

God of love,
you share your life with us in your Son
and bring us to delight in love.
Bless (*N* and *N*)
as they commit themselves to one another today.
Keep them faithful and true,
sustain them through times of sorrow and joy,
deepen their union in heart and body
that they may be to each other a gift of blessing.
Bring them at the end of their lives
to rejoice in the fulfilment of your eternal promises,
through Jesus Christ, our friend and brother. Amen.

Wedding/marriage

Lord of love,
you bring bridegroom and bride together
to share in the delight and tenderness
of passionate embrace and intimate journey.
Give to all joined in marriage
the gifts of patience and kindness,
forbearance and endurance,
faithfulness and loyalty,
considerate understanding and honour,
that they may be a joyful gift to one another
and grow enriched in mind, body and spirit,
through Jesus Christ, our beloved Lord and Saviour. Amen.

Expectant mothers

God, whose brooding Spirit moved over the waters
and caused life to come into being,
bless all who have new life growing within them.
We thank you for the mystery
that brings us to delight and share in your creating work.
To those expectant of your promise,
bring hope to birth and rejoicing;
through Jesus Christ. Amen.

New parents

Lord Jesus Christ,
Mary and Joseph knew excitement and rejoicing
at your birth.
Bless all new parents as they celebrate the arrival
of their children.
Give them the gifts of your grace
to nurture, protect and set their children
on sure foundations,
that, inspired by truth and emotionally secure,
they may flourish to become all
that you would have them be. Amen.

Mothering Sunday

God, whose brooding Spirit brings life to birth
and in Christ restores us to new life,
bless all mothers as they care for their families.
Feed them as they nourish and sustain;
strengthen them as they protect and shelter;
embrace them as they love and cherish,
that children may grow on secure foundations
and all may flourish to your honour and glory. Amen.

Father's Day

God our Father,
through your grace we are adopted as your children
and heirs of eternal life.
Bless all fathers in the care and nurture of their children.
Give them love that will never let go,
compassion to guide and encourage,
wisdom to inspire and delight in growth.
Heal any injuries which might otherwise blight intimacy,
and bring us all together as members of your family;
through your Son Jesus Christ, our brother and Saviour.
Amen.

Betrayal

Lord Jesus Christ,
you endured betrayal from one close to you
who had shared your food
and enjoyed your company and confidence.
Heal the hurts of abused trust that injure us
when those whom we called friend have betrayed intimacy.
We thank you for those who help us
rediscover how to trust again
and open our guard to love that sets us free.
Give us grace to trust in your unfailing love,
now and always. Amen.

Divorce and separation

Lord of life and love,
for everything there is a season:
a time to embrace
and a time to refrain from embracing;
a time to laugh
and a time to cry;
a time to walk together
and a time to walk apart.
Forgive the failures
that have fractured the union made,
the rending asunder
of the bond we prayed no one would divide,
the pains endured
and the hurts inflicted.
Give grace to find anew
the path of life and hope,
that in your peace
we may find true wholeness and joy,
through Jesus Christ our Lord. Amen.

FOOD AND HOSPITALITY

Graces

Before a banquet

Bountiful God,
from your abundance
we are able to participate in your goodness.
Open our hearts to all in need.
As we enjoy this banquet
so may we delight in your provision
and show that thankfulness in lives of justice and equality,
through Jesus Christ,
who shared the company of rich and poor alike. Amen.

Before a Christmas dinner

Christ, in whose name we celebrate this season
with hospitality, joy and music,
bless all who gather round tables this night
to share of your goodness.
We thank you for the gifts we enjoy
to sustain us in body and relationships,
charity and hope.
May we show the generosity of your bounty
in lives of grace and truth,
to the honour of your holy name,
now and for ever. Amen.

Before a dinner

God of unity,
you call us round your table
and we meet you in the breaking of bread.
May the hospitality we enjoy
draw us into a deeper fellowship
with one another and with you.
Give us thankful hearts for all your goodness,
and may we show those thanks in lives of humble service;
through Jesus Christ our Lord. Amen.

Before a meal

Bless, O Lord, this food we are about to eat;
may it be good for our body and soul.
As we are thankful so make us mindful
of all that has produced it,
of those with whom we will share it,
of those who would taste but a morsel of it;
that your peace may be our peace,
and your generosity inspire a generous spirit within us;
through Jesus Christ our Lord. Amen.

Hospitality

Lord, by the oaks of Mamre
you shared Abraham's food;
on the green grass
you fed crowds who flocked to hear your Son,
and in the upper room
you made sharing bread and wine
to be the memorial of your transforming love.
Bless us in the hospitality we show to friends and strangers.
May the unknown guests be to us angels and Christ himself.
Keep us ever thankful for your overflowing generosity
that our lives may proclaim your praise,
and bless all who would share our table. Amen.

Chocolate

Lord God,
you delight us with taste and smell
and set us on the earth
with a rich bounty of plants and fruits.
We give you thanks for chocolate,
its sensuous textures and stimulation,
for the pleasure of giving and the joy of receiving it.
May our enjoyment not be marred
by any means of its production;
rather may the love it expresses and engenders
embrace all,
to your honour and glory. Amen.

Wine

Lord, you gave wine
as a symbol of rejoicing in your Kingdom,
of overflowing goodness
and of your own life poured out for us.
As it is shared,
may we delight in your generous love
that draws friends, lovers and strangers
into your company.
Bring us with joy
to your eternal banquet
where all are united
in one praise and glory. Amen.

Beer

Lord, in your wonderful mystery
you have given us the ability
to turn grain and hops into beer and ale.
Bless the company in which it is shared
and the relaxation it brings.
Keep us from excessive consumption and behaviour.
Lead us to delight in your good provision,
now and always. Amen.

DEVOTIONAL PRAYERS

Still my restless heart, O God

Still my restless heart, O God,
that I may breathe your love.
Still my restless mind, O God,
that I may hear you speak.
Still my restless body, O God,
that I may know you are near.
Still my restless desires, O God,
that I may feel your love.
Still my restless spirit, O God,
that I may trust your will.
Still my restless work, O God,
that I may receive your grace.
In your peace may I find true blessing
through Jesus Christ. Amen.

Stir us, O God

Stir us, O God, with your vibrant desire.
Move us, O God, to work for your justice.
Inspire us, O God, to active service.
Keep us, O God, from complacent indifference.
Challenge us, O God, with your compassion and mercy.
Take and shape us, O God,
to live and love as your Son, Jesus Christ. Amen.

Pilgrims on earth

God, who led the children of Israel through the wilderness
by a cloud by day and a fire by night,
guide us in our earthly pilgrimage.
Inspire us with your truth,
direct us in your justice
and keep us from losing our way in word and deed.
Bring us to the goal of your promise
where blessing finds fulfilment and hope is complete;
through Jesus Christ our Lord. Amen.

Like children

Give us the eyes of a child, O God,
to delight in your world.
May we see your wonders anew,
hear the sounds of joy and laughter,
and discover as we play the majesty of your glory.
Keep us from closing our hearts
through arrogance and pride.
Open us to the praise that excites the soul,
through Jesus Christ. Amen.

Spiritual struggle

Lord Jesus Christ,
in the garden you struggled
with accepting the sacrificial path.
Sustain us in our struggles
where the way is hard and beyond what we can bear.
Send your Spirit
to strengthen our resolve to do your will,
to drink the cup that you drink
and find in our cross the way of life and peace;
to the glory of God the Father. Amen.

Letting go

God of hope, you hold us all our days.
Give us courage to let go of all that would hold us back
and weigh us down on our journey.
Move us on to embrace the future you lay before us,
to step out in faith and trust into the unknown.
Calm our fear,
and strengthen us for all that is hard to leave
and will be missed.
Give us grace to rejoice
with thankful hearts in your love
that is always with us
and never loosens its grip;
through Jesus Christ our Lord. Amen.

Five senses

Feed me, Lord, with your eternal Word;
Touch me, Lord, with your loving embrace;
Awaken me, Lord, with the sounds of your music;
Refresh me, Lord, with the scent of your grace;
Inspire me, Lord, with the sight of your glory. Amen.

April Fools (1)

God of the lowly and outcasts,
your Son chose to be with the rejected,
the unclean and the despised.
May your foolishness,
which is wiser than human wisdom,
confront us with truths unseen,
puncture our overinflated pride
and sharpen our distorted vision,
that the dignity of all may be restored
and your face be seen
in those the world considers to be of little worth;
through Jesus Christ. Amen.

April Fools (2)

Give us courage, Lord Christ,
to risk being misunderstood for your sake;
to reach out to those whom to be with may bring scandal,
to dare to speak for justice when advantage calls for silence;
to let go in trust
when fear and prudence counsels keeping hold,
for your profligate love expends itself to the cross
and more gloriously in the resurrection.
Make us fools in your image and for your glory. Amen.

Christ be my light

Christ be my light,
my hope, my way.

Christ be my shield
in the darkest day.

Christ be my song
of joy and delight.

Christ be my steps
through day and night.

Christ be my peace
within my heart.

Christ be my all
and never depart.

Silence into God

In stilled silence I wait on God.
The silence of eternity to enfold me.
The deep silence of the unknowing to absorb me.
The silence of all senses to overwhelm me.
Bring me, O Lord, at the last
to oneness with the silence of your heart;
for you are the source and goal
of all that I am and shall be. Amen.

Expectation

Risen Lord,
in the early morning light
Mary heard you call her by name.
May our hearts rejoice in your praise
and our vision be transformed
to be expectant with your glory,
now and always. Amen.

Slowness to believe

Lord of resurrection,
the sight of your Son's grave-clothes
was enough to convince his disciple of his rising.
Forgive the slowness of our faith
and our doubting of your power;
for nothing is impossible with you,
who caused all to come into being,
and will bring everything
to fulfil the purposes of your love
in Jesus Christ. Amen.

Doubt and faith

Risen Lord,
behind closed doors
you turned Thomas's doubt
into a shout of faith.
Take our questioning minds
and make them a gateway
to hope and trust in you,
that faith may seek
and find understanding
in your mysterious purposes and will;
for your honour and glory. Amen.

Open a space, O God

Open a space, O God,
where I may know you are near.

Open a space, O God,
where your trust may penetrate my heart.

Open a space, O God,
where hope may be renewed.

Open a space, O God,
where souls may touch
and kindness kindle compassion.

Open a space, O God,
when sinners may find release from the chains of guilt
and all may grow to rejoice in your love. Amen.

Waves (trust in God)

Keep me afloat, O Lord,
as the waves crash around and over me,
threatening to overwhelm.
Be my constant and sure ground
as the tide of time ebbs and flows,
bringing new surprises and challenges to my shore.
Cleanse and refresh my soul
as the beach is renewed
by the incoming waters.
Make my hope soar
as the birds in flight,
and give me a song of praise
to rejoice in your goodness
in Jesus Christ. Amen.

Ripon Jewel (true treasure)

Precious is your love, dear Lord;
as gold does not tarnish,
so you are constant and true.
As gems sparkle in your light,
so do our hearts
when filled with your radiant goodness.
As craftsmen's skill and artistry fashions splendour,
so may we be shaped for your service.
Keep us from false treasures,
that beauty may point to godliness
and delight us with a foretaste of heaven;
for in your glory is our hope and salvation,
through Jesus Christ our Lord. Amen.

A general thanksgiving

Thanks be to God
for love that gives us life
and holds us through all our days.

Thanks be to God
for friends who share our joys and sorrows,
and in whose company we can delight and flourish.

Thanks be to God
for food and shelter,
sufficient for the day.

Thanks be to God
for knowledge and learning,
uncovering the mysteries of your glory in creation.

Thanks be to God
for music and the arts lifting our spirits,
and opening the depths of our being.

Thanks be to God
for the hope of heaven
in your Son Jesus Christ. Amen.

This day

Give me grace, O Christ,
for this day,
that I may be a person of
praise and thanksgiving,
rejoicing and delight,
compassion and understanding.
May I be blessing to all I meet
and be blessed in them;
for your name's sake. Amen.

Index of themes

154